LIVING IN
NORTH & SOUTH
AMERICA

Living in
BRAZIL

Jen Green

W
FRANKLIN WATTS
LONDON • SYDNEY

Franklin Watts
First published in Great Britain in 2016 by The Watts Publishing Group

Copyright © The Watts Publishing Group, 2016

Credits
Series Editor: Julia Bird
Editor: Sarah Silver
Series Design: D.R. ink

ISBN 978 1 4451 4874 8

Picture credits: Africa Images/istockphoto: 16t. Caterina Belova/Shutterstock: front cover, 19t. bonchan/Shutterstock: 15t. BrazilPhoto/Shutterstock: 16b. Briansil/Shutterstock: 10t. ckchui/Shutterstock: 13b. Daniel M Ernst/Shutterstock: 8t. Ma Felipe/istockphoto: 12t. Felipe Frazao/Dreamstime: 5t. Felipe Frazao/Shutterstock: 7t, 20t. Natali Glado/Shutterstock: 13t, 23t. Robert Harding PL/Superstock: 6b. ImagoPhoto/Shutterstock: 18t. JAG Images/Alamy: 14t. JBK/Shutterstock: 15b. Florian Kopp/Imagebroker/Superstock: 9tl, 17b. Eduardo Leite /istockphoto: 4t. Giancarlo Liguori/Shutterstock: 8b. Luizouzarj/Dreamstime: 21b. Guenter Manaus/Shutterstock: 19b. Marcello74/Shutterstock: 6t, 9tr. Edward Marques/Dreamstime: 21t. Carlos Mora/Dreamstime: 5b. Carlos Neto/Shutterstock: 12b. Guenter Purin/Shutterstock: 18b. Alf Ribero/Shutterstock: 11t, 20b. A. Ricardo/Shutterstock: 17t Sjors737/Dreamstime: 7b. Snehitdesign/Dreamstime: 10b. Robin Tenison/Robert Harding PL: 11b. Beth Wolff43/istockphoto: 14b. Gary Yim/Shutterstock: 9bl.

MIX
Paper from
responsible sources
FSC® C104740
www.fsc.org

Printed in China

Franklin Watts
An imprint of
Hachette Children's Group
Part of The Watts Publishing Group
Carmelite House
50 Victoria Embankment
London EC4Y 0DZ

An Hachette UK Company
www.hachette.co.uk

www.franklinwatts.co.uk

Contents

Words in bold are in the glossary on page 23.

Welcome to Brazil

Hi! I come from Brazil. It is a very large country in South America.

Venezuela
Guyana
French Guiana
Suriname
Atlantic Ocean
Amazon River
The Amazon Rainforest
BRAZIL
Peru
BRASÍLIA
Bolivia
RIO DE JANEIRO
Paraguay
SÃO PAULO
Pacific Ocean
Chile
Argentina
Uruguay

Location

Brazil covers nearly half of South America. It is the fifth-largest country in the world. Brazil shares **borders** with ten countries. It also has a very long coastline on the Atlantic Ocean.

the Amazon River

Landscapes

Brazil's scenery is famous the world over. The mighty Amazon River runs across northern Brazil. It flows through the Amazon Rainforest, which is bigger than any other rainforest. There are also hills and mountains, flat **plains**, sandy beaches and wetlands.

Weather

Brazil has a **tropical climate**, with warm or hot conditions all year round. The mountains are cooler in winter. Rain falls all year round in the Amazon Rainforest. Other places have a dry and a rainy season.

A tropical storm blows across a beach in the north of Brazil.

People of Brazil

We're from Brazil. Our country has over 200 million people. That's nearly half of all the people in South America.

Many peoples

People from many different countries live in Brazil. The first people of Brazil were rainforest groups, called **Amerindians**. In 1500, Portuguese explorers arrived and Brazil became a Portuguese **colony**. For 300 years, the Portuguese ruled Brazil. They brought in African slaves to work on large farms called **plantations**.

The Yanomami are a group of Amerindians who live in the Amazon Rainforest.

Far and wide

In 1822, Brazil became an **independent** country. After that, more people came to settle here. They came from European countries, such as Germany, Italy and Spain. They also arrived from the **Middle East** and Asian countries, such as China and Japan.

Brazil is sometimes called a melting pot, because people from so many different places live here.

Language

Portuguese is Brazil's **official language**. Many other languages are spoken here too.

Brazilian children reading in a village

Cities

Brazil has many cities. Nearly all of them lie on or near the coast. I come from Rio de Janeiro on the southeast coast.

São Paulo

São Paulo is Brazil's largest city. With over ten million people, it's one of the world's biggest cities. People travel to the centre to work in offices, factories, shops and markets.

São Paulo's city centre is very crowded, with many tall buildings.

Rio

Rio de Janeiro is the second-largest city. We just call it Rio. Nearby is a tall, pointed mountain called Sugarloaf Mountian. A giant statue of Jesus Christ stands on top of another mountain, Corcovado.

Sugarloaf Mountain

Brasília was built in the shape of a plane or flying bird. You can see this shape from the air.

Brasília

Brasília is the **capital** of Brazil. Rio used to be the capital, but in the 1950s, the government decided the capital should be nearer the centre of our huge country. Brasília was built in just four years and opened in 1960. It has many unusual buildings, including a cathedral shaped like a spiky crown.

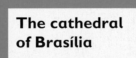

The cathedral of Brasília

Town and country life

Fifty years ago, most Brazilians lived in the country, but now most people live in cities. Our cities have grown quickly as people move in from the countryside.

Rich and poor

Brazil's cities have rich people, but most people are poor. Poor people live on the outskirts, in slums called **favelas**. I live in a favela outside São Paulo. Our home is made of wood and sheet metal. There is no electricity and many families share a tap.

Favelas in São Paulo

Farms and mines

In the country, most people work as farmers. Many work on big plantations, growing crops, such as coffee and **sugar cane**. Others work on ranches where beef cattle are raised, or have their own small farms. Some people work as miners, but the **mining** life is hard.

coffee beans

Rainforest people

Some Amerindian groups live deep in the rainforest. They live by hunting animals and growing crops in small clearings. Some groups have little or no contact with the outside world.

A Yanomami man digging in the forest

Scenery and wildlife

Brazil is a beautiful country with many different landscapes. Rainforests, wetlands, grassy plains and coasts all have their own wildlife.

Mighty river

The Amazon is the world's second-longest river. It flows right across Brazil to the Atlantic Ocean. The mouth of the river is very wide. The Amazon contains more water than any other river in the world.

A boat floats down the wide Amazon River.

A colourful toucan in the rainforest

Rainforest

The river acts as a highway through the dense Amazon Rainforest. But parts of the forest are being cut down for timber or to make way for new villages, mines and farms.

The Amazon Rainforest has an amazing variety of wildlife. Scientists have counted 40,000 different plants and 1,300 types of bird.

capybaras

Wetland

The Pantanal is a huge wetland the size of France. During the rainy season it turns into a vast lake! There are crocodiles, sharp-toothed fish called piranhas, and capybaras, which are giant **rodents**.

What we eat

People from different countries have brought their own cooking to Brazil. The result is that our food is varied – and very tasty!

coconuts

Basic foods

Most Brazilians mainly live on beans, rice and **manioc**. This starchy root must be grated and cooked as flour before you eat it. Many dishes contain a little fish or meat. Sometimes we grill meat on the barbecue for a treat!

Preparing manioc flour

feijoada

Tastes of Africa

Many of our favourite dishes come from Africa. *Feijoada* is a stew made with black beans, dried beef and pork. It is eaten with fried manioc flour and sliced oranges. *Acarajé* are balls of mashed black-eyed peas. They are deep-fried in palm oil and stuffed with spicy shrimp paste.

Purple acai berries are made into fruit juice and ice cream. These juicy berries come from palm trees.

Brazilian foods abroad

Brazilian farmers grow a lot of food that is sold abroad. Brazilian coffee, sugar, nuts, oranges and beef are eaten and drunk all over the world.

Having fun

Brazilians are mad about sport! My favourite sports are football and swimming.

Football

Our national sport is football. We are very proud of our national team, which has won the World Cup five times. That's more times than any other team. Brazil's top players are known for their skill and style.

playing football

Pelé

Pelé (born in 1940) is one of the world's most famous football players. He helped to win three World Cups and scored a total of 1,281 goals, making him the most successful league goal scorer ever.

Playing volleyball on a beach in Rio

Outdoor fun

Brazilians spend a lot of time outdoors in the warm sunshine. Basketball, volleyball and tennis are popular. We also like to watch motor racing and horse racing. People keep fit by jogging and working out.

Fighting art

Capoeira is a unique Brazilian sport. It's a mixture of fighting, dance, acrobatics and music. People form a ring to watch the contest in the middle.

A capoeira contest

Famous places

Brazil is a great country to visit. There are lots of amazing places to see, but the country is so big, it takes a long time to see all of it!

the Iguaçu Falls

Waterfalls

Iguaçu Falls is one of the world's most beautiful waterfalls. It lies on the border with Argentina. The river drops 72 metres in a huge horseshoe-shaped falls. Giant otters live in Iguaçu National Park.

Copacabana beach

Beaches

Brazil has one of the longest coastlines in the world. There are many white, sandy beaches. The most famous is Copacabana beach in Rio. People head for the beach to go swimming, diving or sailing, or just to relax.

The opera house in Manaus is called the Amazon Theatre.

Manaus

The city of Manaus is the capital of the Amazon region. It stands on the banks of the Amazon River. In the 19th century, it was the centre of the rubber trade. Manaus grew very wealthy because rubber was in demand to make car tyres. The city has many grand buildings, including an opera house. The city is a good base for a trip to the rainforest.

Festivals and holidays

Brazil has many **festivals** and holidays. Some are religious days, others celebrate important dates in our history. There's always something to celebrate!

Religion

Most Brazilians are Roman Catholic. The Portuguese brought this religion to Brazil five hundred years ago. There are also many Protestants. Some people follow an African religion called **Candomblé**.

A Catholic procession in São Paulo

Carnival time

Carnival is our most famous festival. It takes place all over Brazil just before **Lent**. The biggest celebrations are in Rio. Musicians and dancers in colourful costumes parade through the streets. There are amazing decorated **floats**. Everyone dances to the rhythms of **samba**, which is Brazilian carnival music. The party goes on for days.

A float in the Rio carnival parade

New Year festival

Followers of Candomblé celebrate New Year's Eve on the beach. They offer flowers and floating candles to honour Iemanjá, the goddess of the sea.

People taking flowers to the sea goddess to celebrate New Year's Eve

Brazil: Fast facts

Capital: Brasília

Population: 200.4 million (2013)

Area: 8.5 million sq km

Official language: Portuguese

Currency: The real

Main religions: Roman Catholicism, Protestantism, Candomblé

Longest river: Amazon, 6,400 km

Highest mountain: Pico da Neblina, 2,995 m

National holidays: New Year's Day (1 January), Carnival (February or March), Good Friday and Easter Sunday, Tiradentes Day (21 April), Labour Day (1 May), Corpus Christi (May or June), Independence Day (7 September), Our Lady of Aparecida (12 October), All Souls' Day (2 November), Republic Day (15 November), Zumbi dos Palmares (20 November), Christmas Day (25 December)

Glossary

Amerindians the original people of Brazil

border a line marking the boundary between two countries

Candomblé a Brazilian religion that is based on African beliefs

capital city where the country's government meets

climate the regular weather pattern in a region

colony a territory ruled by another country

favela a Brazilian word for a slum

festival a celebration, usually for religious reasons

float a decorated vehicle that carries people in a parade

Lent the forty days before Easter

manioc a root crop that is also known as cassava

Middle East an area that covers southeast Asia and northwest Africa

mining digging out materials, such as coal or precious metals, from the ground

official language the main language of a country that is approved by the government

plain an area of low, flat land

plantation a large farm where crops, such as coffee, rubber or sugar cane are grown.

rodent a type of small mammal with large, sharp front teeth; mice, rats and hamsters are rodents

samba a Brazilian dance

sugar cane a tropical grass from which sugar is made

tropical belonging to the tropics, the area around the Equator

Index

A

Africa 6, 15, 20, 21
Amazon Rainforest 4, 5, 13
Amazon River 4, 5, 22
Amerindians 6, 11
Atlantic Ocean 4, 12

B

beach 5, 17, 19, 21
borders 4, 18
Brasília 4, 9, 22

C

capoeira 17
carnival 21, 22
cities 8–9, 10, 19
climate 5
coast 4, 8, 12, 19
colony 6
country 10–11

D

dance 17, 21

E

Europe 4, 7

F

farming 6, 11, 13, 15
favela 10
festivals 20–21
food 11, 14–15
football 16

H

holidays 20–21, 22
homes 10

I

Independence Day 22

L

lakes 13
landscape 4, 12, 13, 18, 19

M

Manaus 19
mountains 5, 9

N

national parks 18

P

plantations 6, 11
poor 10
population 6, 8, 22
Portuguese 6, 7, 20, 22

R

rainforest 4, 5, 6, 11, 12, 13, 19
religion 20, 21
rich 10
Rio de Janeiro 4, 8, 9
rivers 4, 5, 12, 13, 18, 22

S

São Paulo 4, 8, 10, 20
settlers 7
slaves 6
sports 16, 17
Sugarloaf 9

T

tropical 5

W

waterfalls 18
wetlands 5, 12, 13
wildlife 12, 13, 18